Generations of visitors have discovered the ocean world through the exhibits and educational programs of the Birch Aquarium at Scripps, the public outreach center for the world-renowned Scripps Institution of Oceanography at UC San Diego. Now our heralded aquarium-museum is offering a new mode of discovery: *What Color Would You Be to Hide in the Sea?*, a stunning children's book inspired by the aquarium's popular exhibit, "The Art of Deception," which has delighted thousands of visitors of all ages since it opened in 2005.

What Color Would You Be to Hide in the Sea? celebrates the often surprising camouflage tactics used by some of the ocean's most beautiful creatures. The book's rich blend of stunning photographs from the aquarium's exhibit, lush watercolors, playful poems, and fascinating science notes offers children and adults alike a chance to see with their own eyes the marine creatures normally hidden deep in the sea.

Created exclusively by the Birch Aquarium at Scripps, this beautiful book helps support our important work. Our mission is to provide ocean science education through creative exhibits, programs, and activities. We interpret Scripps Institution of Oceanography research, emphasizing the interdisciplinary nature of the science used to study the oceans and the Earth and inspiring public support of scientific endeavors. We also promote conservation through education and research, believing that with increased understanding of the oceans, people will respect and protect the marine environment. *What Color Would You Be to Hide in the Sea?* is one more creative way we're bringing people and the ocean closer together.

Nigella Hillgarth
Executive Director of Birch Aquarium
Scripps Institution of Oceanography
University of California San Diego

What Color

to

A Birch Aquarium at Scripps Book

BIRCH AQUARIUM
Scripps Institution of Oceanography
UC San Diego

Would You Be Hide in the Sea?

Master of Disguise

Octopus, master of disguise.
When it comes to hiding, you fool the eyes . . .

    You change your color to fit your mood,
    Or to hide yourself as you hunt for food.

    When changing color is not enough,
    You switch your texture from smooth to rough.

    To fake out hunters, you show four eyes.
    Just two are real; two are disguise.

    If sharks or eels still aim your way,
    You squirt dark ink then swish away.

Octopus, you are alive
Because your disguises help you survive.

Two-spot octopus

Looking Leafy

Leafy fish, sneaky fish.
    Among seaweed you live.
    In seaweed you hide.
    From seaweed you strike.
Leafy fish, sneaky fish.

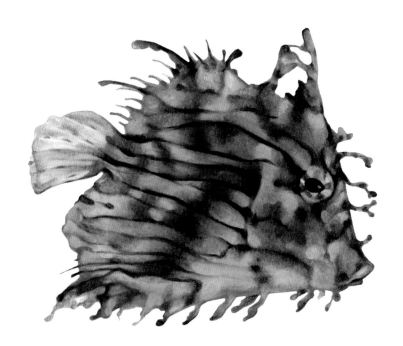

Leafy filefish

SNEAKY SURVIVAL STRATEGIES

Break It Up
Stripes and spots break up the outline of an animal's body. This fish has both.

Sailfin tang

Blend In
Animals colored to blend with their surroundings can hide in the open. Can you find the fish in this picture?

Peacock sole

Fake It
Black spots near the tail resemble eyes, perhaps confusing predators about which end is which. Where is this fish's real eye?

Threadfin butterflyfish

e a Copy Cat

his tasty filefish
ooks enough like a
oisonous pufferfish
o discourage
redators. Would
ou be able to tell
hem apart?

Mimic filefish

Valentinni's sharpnose puffer

Warty frogfish

Act the Part

The body shape, skin color and
texture, and the ability to sit still
help the frogfish imitate a sponge-
encrusted rock. Would you be fooled?

Dress It Up

Decorator crabs camouflage
hemselves by attaching bits of
heir habitat to their body. There
eally IS a crab in this picture!

Decorator crab

Hornyhead turbot

Flat Is Where It's At

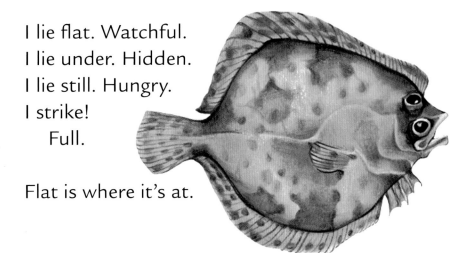

I lie flat. Watchful.
I lie under. Hidden.
I lie still. Hungry.
I strike!
    Full.

Flat is where it's at.

Red lionfish

Hungry Reef Hunter

Hungry lionfish prowls the reef
With bold colors beyond belief,
Hunting for a meal.

Hunting
Lionfish corners its prey,
Spiny fins blocking the way.

Hunting
Gathered into a tight bunch,
Prey is about to become lunch!

Hunting
With a lightning-fast jab,
Lionfish makes a quick grab.

Hungry lionfish prowls the reef
With bold colors beyond belief,
Hunting for a meal.

WHAT COLOR WOULD YOU BE TO HIDE IN THE SEA?

Cabezon

How do you feel
about red?
It works on a scarlet
anemone bed.

Would being yellow
help?
Yes . . . if you hang
around giant kelp.

Giant kelpfish

Robust ghost pipefish

Might orange fit you
well?
If a sponge of that hue
is where you dwell.

Blue shark

What about green?
Hiding in seagrass,
you might not be
seen.

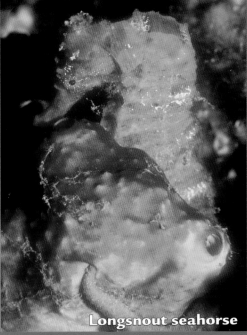

Longsnout seahorse

Ever thought about
blue?
Animals hide in the
open sea, too!

Seahorse Secrets

Pipefish and seahorses blend in with the scenery,
Matching sponges, sea fans, or even sea greenery.
For animals like this, that aren't so quick,
Camouflage sure is a useful trick.

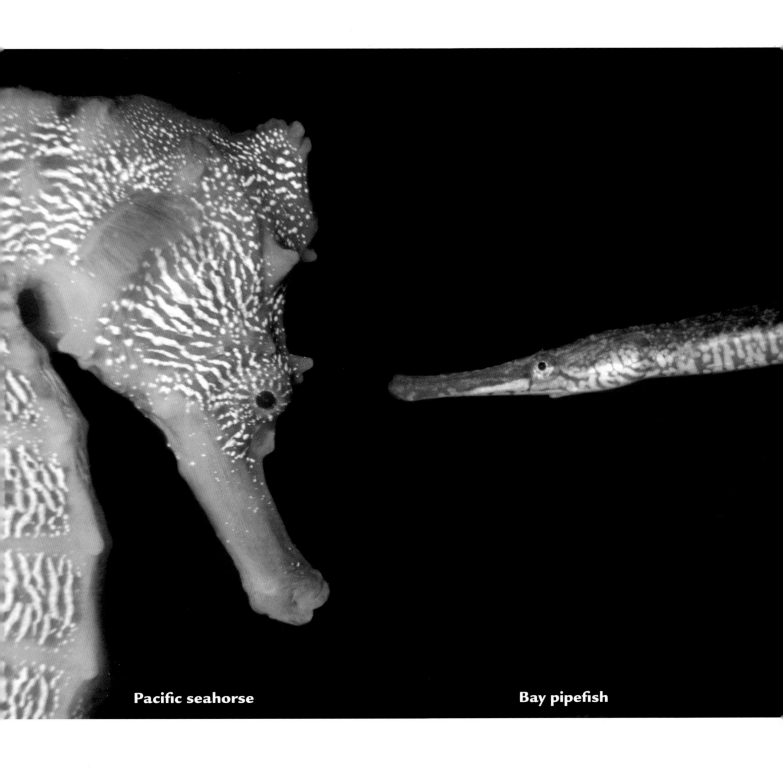

Pacific seahorse   **Bay pipefish**

Leafy seadragon

Floating Dragon

Leafy seadragon floating by,
I can't help but wonder why
You hide among the weeds so brown,
Even when no one's around?

Leafy seadragon floating by,
What small creature caught your eye?
You move your head—fast and quick!—
To catch a mysid lickety-split.

Leafy seadragon floating by,
You are elusive, it's no lie.
Just when I think I spy you here
Into the weeds you disappear.

Some animals hide their real eyes; others have fake "eyes" to disguise or surprise.

Why Hide the Eye?

Eyes can give animals away, whether they're hunting or being hunted. Many fishes hide their eyes in dark stripes or complex patterns.

Redtail butterflyfish

Lacy scorpionfish

Emperor angelfish

Bluelashed butterflyfish

Peacock sole

Emperor angelfish (juvenile

Goldengirdled coralfish

Heads or Tails?

... black spot near
... e tail may appear
... be an eye, luring a
... redator to attack the
... rong end of its prey.

Can Eyes Lie About Size?

... arge false "eyespots"
... n a small fish may
... ool would-be
... redators into
... hinking the animal is
... igger than it really is.

Epaulette shark

Two-spot octopus

Ornate ghost pipefish

Are You Seeing Red?

How can a fish hide if it's fire-engine red?
You might think it better to be drab instead.
But red's not so bright in deep waters blue,
(And it helps to hang out near a red sea fan, too.)

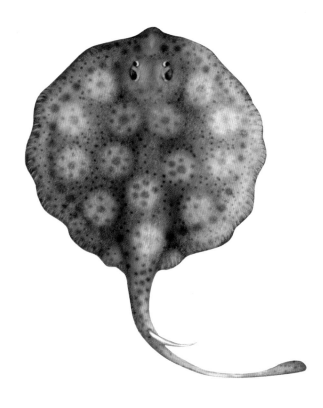

The Ways of Rays

Flutter your disk, stingray,
To whisk the sand away.
For beneath it lies
To probing eyes . . .
 Clams!
A tasty feast today.

Lie under the sand, stingray,
To hide in your special way.
A sunny beach.
Watch for feet!
 Sting!
Flutter, quick, get away.

Oh, the fluttery ways of rays.

Round stingray

Pacific sardine

One way to survive in the deep blue soup
is to swim about in a shimmering group.

Backs that are dark and undersides light
help open-sea creatures fade from sight.

VANISHING TRICKS IN THE OPEN OCEAN

Blue shark

Moon jelly

Drifters like jellies are clear;
being see-through helps them disappear.

Camouflage is an essential survival strategy, both on land and in the ocean. It helps prey to escape detection and predators to sneak up on prey. The marine animals in this book camouflage themselves in a variety of undersea habitats including rocky reef, coral reef, kelp forest, sandy seafloor, and open ocean. Here are more facts about each of those animals.

Blue shark   pages 2–3, 15, 26–27
Prionace glauca
Size: up to 13 ft. (4 m)
Range: worldwide in temperate and subtropical seas
Habitat: open ocean
Diet: fishes, squid

Photo © David Hinkel

Blue sharks are adapted for a wide-ranging life in the open ocean and may travel long distances. Their split coloration is called countershading. When viewed from above, their blue back helps them disappear against the dark depths. Viewed from below, their white belly blends with sunlit waters.

Sailfin tang   page 8
Zebrasoma veliferum
Size: up to 16 in. (40 cm)
Range: tropical Pacific Ocean
Habitat: coral reefs
Diet: algae

Photo © Robert Burhans

The sailfin tang feeds during the day and hides in the reef at night to avoid predators. Stripes, like those of a zebra, help to break up the outline of the animal's body. This type of camouflage is known as disruptive coloration. Sharp spines at the base of the tail may also be used to fend off predators.

Peacock sole
pages 8 and 20
Pardachirus pavoninus
Size: up to 10 in. (25 cm)
Range: tropical Indo-Pacific Ocean
Habitat: sandy and muddy bottoms
Diet: small crustaceans

Photo © David Hi

With so many dark and light spots on its body, the peacock sole disappears against the ocean floor. Flat and round, it's hard to tell where this fish ends and the sand begins.

Photo © David Hi

Warty frogfish   page 9
Antennarius maculatus
Size: up to 6 in. (15 cm)
Range: tropical Indo-Pacific Ocean
Habitat: coral reefs
Diet: small fishes, crustaceans

Photo © Marie Tartar

The frogfish is truly a master of disguise. When sitting still, its lumpy body looks just like the sponges it lives around. On its head, the frogfish has a long spine with a tuft of tissue at the end that it uses like a fishing pole. It dangles the fleshy "lure" to attract small fishes and shrimp, then gobbles them up.

Decorator crab   page 9
Loxorhynchus crispatus
Size: up to 5 in. (13 cm)
Range: Eastern Pacific Ocean: northern California
Habitat: rocky reefs, kelp forests
Diet: small shrimp, zooplankton

Photo © Mary Ros

Decorator crabs attach bits of algae and smal animals such as sea anemones and sponges to small hooks (setae) on their backs and legs. E when moving, they look more like a rock than crab!

-spot octopus   pages 5 and 21

pus bimaculatus

: up to 2 ft. (61 cm)

ge: Eastern Pacific Ocean: southern California to
Baja California, Mexico

itat: low tide zone and nearshore waters, under rocks
and on mudflats

t: clams, mussels, crabs, small fishes

Photo © Tracy Clark   Photo © Steve Eilenberg

two-spot octopus gets its name from the large, dark spot under each of its eyes.
se false "eyespots" are larger than the real eyes, which may help the octopus seem bigger
n it is to discourage predators. This species is generally dark red but can change its skin color
texture to match its surroundings.

Leafy filefish   page 7

Chaetodermis penicilligerus

Size: up to 12 in. (30 cm)

Range: tropical Indo-West
Pacific Ocean

Habitat: weed-covered
bottoms near coral reefs

Diet: small invertebrates

Photo © Robert Fenner

The body of the leafy filefish is covered with fleshy
tassels that sway back and forth with the water
currents. Brown to brownish-yellow mottling and
horizontal brown lines complete this fish's "weedy"
disguise. A sluggish swimmer, it is often observed
drifting head down in seaweed.

---

eadfin butterflyfish
e 8

etodon auriga

: up to 9 in. (23 cm)

ge: tropical Indo-
Pacific Ocean

itat: coral reefs

t: sea anemones, coral
polyps, algae

Photo © Donal Hill

many butterflyfishes, the eyes of the
eadfin butterflyfish are masked in a black
De. To further confuse predators about which
is the head, this fish has a black spot that
ks like an eye near its tail.

Mimic filefish   page 9

Paraluteres prionurus

Size: up to 4 in. (10 cm)

Range: tropical Indo-West
Pacific Ocean

Habitat: coral reefs

Diet: small snails, algae

If looking just like a
poisonous pufferfish (Valentinni's sharpnose
puffer) isn't enough to scare off would-be
predators, the mimic filefish can raise a spine
behind its head. The spine locks in place, making
the fish a prickly bite.

Photo © Robert Fenner

Valentinni's sharpnose
puffer   page 9

Canthigaster valentini

Size: up to 4 in. (10 cm)

Range: tropical Indo-West
Pacific Ocean

Habitat: coral reefs

Diet: algae, sea squirts, coral
polyps, bryozoans, mollusks

Photo © Robert Fenner

Pufferfishes are named for their ability to swell to
three times their normal size by pumping water
into their stomach. They also produce a toxin that
makes them highly poisonous for other fishes and
humans to eat.

---

rnyhead turbot
e 10

ronichthys verticalis

: up to 15 in. (38 cm)

ge: Eastern Pacific
Ocean: central
California to southern
Baja California, Mexico,
including Gulf of California

itat: sand and mud bottoms

t: crustaceans, worms

Photo © Herb Gruenhagen

bots look and swim like typical fishes at birth.
about six months of age, they change their
style, lying on their side on the seafloor. At this
e, one eye (usually the left) migrates to meet
other so that both eyes are on the upper side
he head.

Red lionfish   page 12

Pterois volitans

Size: up to 15 in. (38 cm)

Range: tropical Indo-West
Pacific Ocean

Habitat: coral reefs

Diet: small fishes, shrimp,
crabs

Photo © Karen Ross-Gibbins

Lionfish raise the many sharp, venomous spines on
their back to defend themselves. These nighttime
hunters find sheltered places to hide and rest
during the day. Their striped color pattern disrupts
the outline of their body and helps them blend in
with their habitat.

Cabezon   page 14

Scorpaenichthys marmoratus

Size: up to 3.3 ft. (1 m)

Range: Eastern Pacific
Ocean: southern Alaska
to central Baja California,
Mexico

Habitat: rock, sand, or mud
bottoms; kelp forests

Diet: fishes, crustaceans, mollusks

Photo © Donal Hill

The cabezon is a powerful suction feeder and
swallows prey whole. It can change its color
from brown to red. Red serves as a warning to
enemies to stay away. The eggs of the cabezon are
poisonous.

EXPLORE MORE, DIVE DEEPER YET

Giant kelpfish page 14

Heterostichus rostratus

Size: up to 2 ft. (61 cm)
Range: Eastern Pacific
Ocean: British Columbia
to southern Baja
California, Mexico
Habitat: rocky reefs with kelp
Diet: shrimp, small fishes

Photo © Donal Hill

The giant kelpfish can change color from green to red to brown to match surrounding seaweed. It often rests nose down. In this position, its body and fins look just like a waving blade of kelp.

Robust ghost pipefish page 15

Solenostomus cyanopterus

Size: up to 6 in. (15 cm)
Range: tropical Indo-West
Pacific Ocean
Habitat: coastal reefs and
weedy areas
Diet: small crustaceans

Photo © Marie Tartar

The robust ghost pipefish could easily pass for a piece of seagrass. This rare species usually occurs in male/female pairs near seaweed or seagrass meadows. Females carry their eggs in a special pouch formed by a pair of fins on their belly. Ghost pipefishes are distant relatives of seahorses.

Longsnout seahorse page 15

Hippocampus reidi

Size: up to 7 in. (18 cm)
Range: tropical western
Atlantic Ocean
Habitat: coral reefs, seagrass
beds
Diet: small crustaceans

Photo © Deanne Edwards

The longsnout seahorse is an Atlantic Ocean cousin of the Pacific seahorse. Like all seahor it is adapted for a slow-moving life and relies camouflage to remain undiscovered. Longsn seahorses often cling to sponges, sea fans, or clumps of seagrass, which they match in colo

Redtail butterflyfish page 20

Chaetodon collare

Size: up to 7 in. (18 cm)
Range: tropical Indo-West
Pacific Ocean
Habitat: coral reefs
Diet: coral polyps, algae,
small crustaceans

Photo © David Hinkel

Vertical stripes of white and black disguise the eyes of the redtail butterflyfish, making it more difficult for predators to attack the head end. With a skinny body and tiny mouth on the end of a thin snout, this fish is well suited for picking food from reef cracks and crevices.

Emperor angelfish page 20

Pomacanthus imperator

Size: up to 15 in. (38 cm)
Range: tropical Indo-Pacific
Ocean
Habitat: coral reefs
Diet: sponges, sea squirts

Photo © Donal Hill

The eyes of the emperor angelfish are hidden by a black mask. Lines of bright blue and yellow break up the outline of its body and help it blend with the brightly colored reef. When predators swim near, the emperor angelfish seeks shelter under ledges and in caves.

Emperor angelfish (juvenile) page 20

Pomacanthus imperator

Size: up to 3 in. (8 cm)
Range: tropical Indo-Pacific
Ocean
Habitat: coral reefs
Diet: sponges, sea squirts

Photo © Robert

As youngsters, emperor angelfish look completely different from their parents. Inste of yellow and blue stripes, they sport a dark blue body with light blue and white rings. Th color gradually begins to change to the adult pattern when they are about 3 inches long.

Epaulette shark page 21

Hemiscyllium ocellatum

Size: up to 3.5 ft. (107 cm)
Range: Western Pacific
Ocean: New Guinea and
northern Australia
Habitat: coral reefs
Diet: bottom-dwelling
invertebrates

Photo © Robert Burhans

With a long, skinny body, the epaulette shark is adapted to hide and hunt in reef cracks and crevices. This small shark has two big, black spots (false "eyespots") just behind its side (pectoral) fins. Since the spots are so much larger than the shark's real eyes, they may fool predators into thinking the shark is bigger than it really is.

Ornate ghost pipefish page 22

Solenostomus paradoxus

Size: up to 4 in. (11 cm)
Range: tropical Indo-West
Pacific Ocean
Habitat: coral reefs
Diet: small crustaceans

Photo © Donal Hill

Ghost pipefish commonly occur in male/female pairs and have a small home range. These amazing fish often float head down, snapping up bottom-dwelling shrimp with their tubelike snout.

Round stingray page 25

Urobatis halleri

Size: up to 22 in. (56 cm)
Range: Eastern Pacific
Ocean: northern
California to Panama
Habitat: sandy and muddy
bottoms
Diet: shrimp, crabs, worms, small fishes

Photo © Tracy Cla

This small stingray is common in shallow coastal waters. Its flat, speckled body blends well with the sandy seafloor. Round stingrays often bury themselves to hide from predators a strategy that also works well for ambushing prey.

...cific seahorse   page 17

...pocampus ingens

...e: up to 12 in. (30 cm)
...ge: Eastern Pacific
  Ocean: southern
  California to Peru,
  including Gulf of
  California

Photo © Greg Ochocki

...bitat: rocky reefs with sea fans; seagrass and
  seaweed beds
...t: small crustaceans

...e Pacific seahorse is the largest known
...horse species. Adapted for a slow-moving
...it often clings to bottom-dwelling plants and
...mals with its long, flexible tail. Seahorses are
...usual because the males brood the eggs in a
...cial pouch and give birth.

Bay pipefish   page 17

Syngnathus leptorhynchus

Size: up to 13 in. (33 cm)
Range: Eastern Pacific
  Ocean: Alaska to
  southern Baja California,
  Mexico
Habitat: eelgrass beds in
  bays and estuaries
Diet: small crustaceans

Photo © Greg Ochocki

In an unusual twist of biology, it's the males that
carry the eggs in a brood pouch under the tail.
Bay pipefish often rest motionless, head down, in
seagrass, where their long, thin bodies mimic the
blades.

Leafy seadragon page 18

Phycodurus eques

Size: up to 14 in. (35 cm)
Range: southern Australia
Habitat: seaweed beds
Diet: small crustaceans

Photo © Mike Byergo

The leafy seadragon is
named for the many leaflike
appendages on its long, slender body. It looks
more like a floating bit of seaweed than a fish. Male
seadragons carry the eggs in special cups on their
tail.

...cy scorpionfish
...ɛ 20

...nopias aphanes

...e: up to 10 in. (25 cm)
...nge: tropical western
  Pacific Ocean
...bitat: coral reefs
...t: crustaceans, small
  fishes

Photo © Deanne Edwards

...th a crazy mazelike color pattern and frilly skin
...sels resembling algae, the lacy scorpionfish
...o well camouflaged on coral reefs that it
...en goes unseen (even by divers!) This ambush
...dator sits still and sucks in prey that venture
...se to its powerful, upturned mouth.

Bluelashed butterflyfish
page 20

Chaetodon bennetti

Size: up to 7 in. (18 cm)
Range: tropical Indo-Pacific
  Ocean
Habitat: coral reefs
Diet: coral polyps

Photo © Donal Hill

Like many butterflyfishes, bluelashed butterflyfish
are often seen swimming around reefs as lone
individuals or in male/female pairs. This species is
easily distinguished by the two blue stripes along
its belly.

Goldengirdled coralfish
page 21

Coradion chrysozonus

Size: up to 6 in. (15 cm)
Range: tropical Indo-West
  Pacific Ocean
Habitat: coral reefs
Diet: sponges

Photo © Donal Hill

The goldengirdled coralfish displays a false
"eyespot" near its tail. Its real eyes are camouflaged
by a black stripe. This coloration may trick
predators into attacking the tail end of the fish,
allowing it to escape more easily.

...cific sardine   page 26

...dinops sagax

...e: up to 16 in. (40 cm)
...nge: Eastern Pacific
  Ocean: Alaska to
  Mexico
...bitat: nearshore waters
  to open ocean
...t: plankton

GoldenStateImages.com
© Randy Morse

...dines are tasty prey for a variety of large fishes
...d marine mammals. Illustrating the notion that
...ere's safety in numbers," they swim in large
...ools for protection from roving predators. If
... school is attacked, flashes of light reflected
...m the sardines' silvery sides as they twist and
...n may blind or distract predators.

Moon jelly   page 27

Aurelia aurita

Size: up to 16 in. (40 cm)
  across
Range: worldwide in
  temperate and tropical
  seas
Habitat: coastal open water
Diet: zooplankton

Photo © Tracy Clark

Like all jellies, moon jellies are weak swimmers.
They move slowly by pulsing their bell, but are
mainly carried along by ocean currents. Moon
jellies sting tiny prey with their fine tentacles.

camouflage

noun • an animal's natural coloring or
  form that enables it to blend in
  with its surroundings

  • actions or devices intended to
  disguise or mislead

verb • hide or disguise the presence
  of an animal by means of
  camouflage

from French, *camoufler* "to disguise"

from Italian, *camuffare* "to disguise or
deceive"

A publication of the Birch Aquarium at Scripps

BIRCH
AQUARIUM
Scripps Institution of Oceanography
UC San Diego

2300 Expedition Way
La Jolla CA 92037
(858) 534-3474
aquarium.ucsd.edu
sio.ucsd.edu

Project directors: Susan Malk, Hei-ock Kim
Science editor: Debbie Zmarzly
Editor: Deborah Halverson
Designer: Kaelin Chappell Broaddus
Watercolor artwork: Eques, Inc.
Writers: Birch Aquarium staff

ISBN 978-0-615-26141-6

Printed in South Korea

Acknowledgements
The Birch Aquarium at Scripps wishes to thank Marty and Russ Ries,
the Birch Aquarium staff, and the amazing photographers who
generously contributed their images to this project.